Holy Night

A Christmas Bible Coloring Book

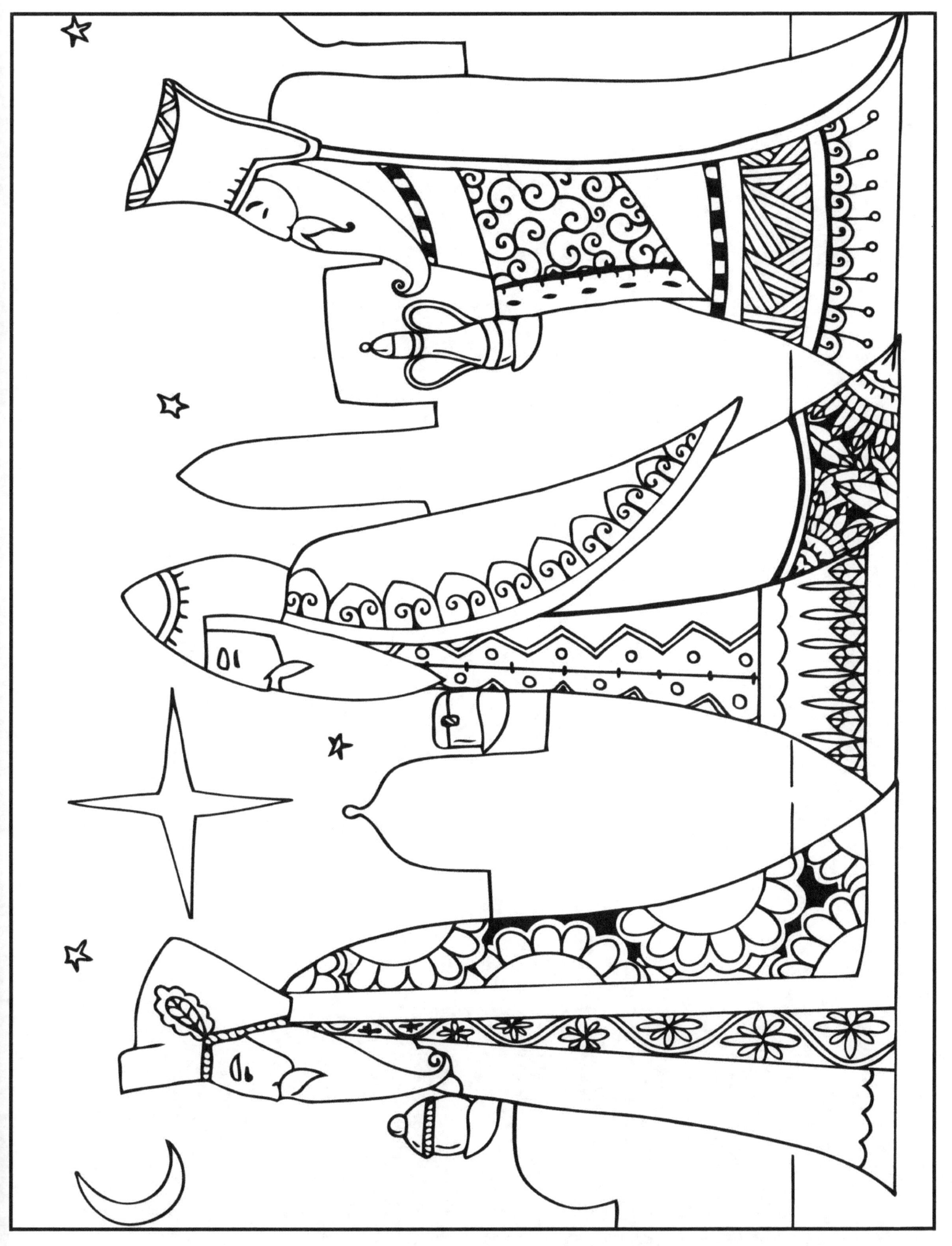

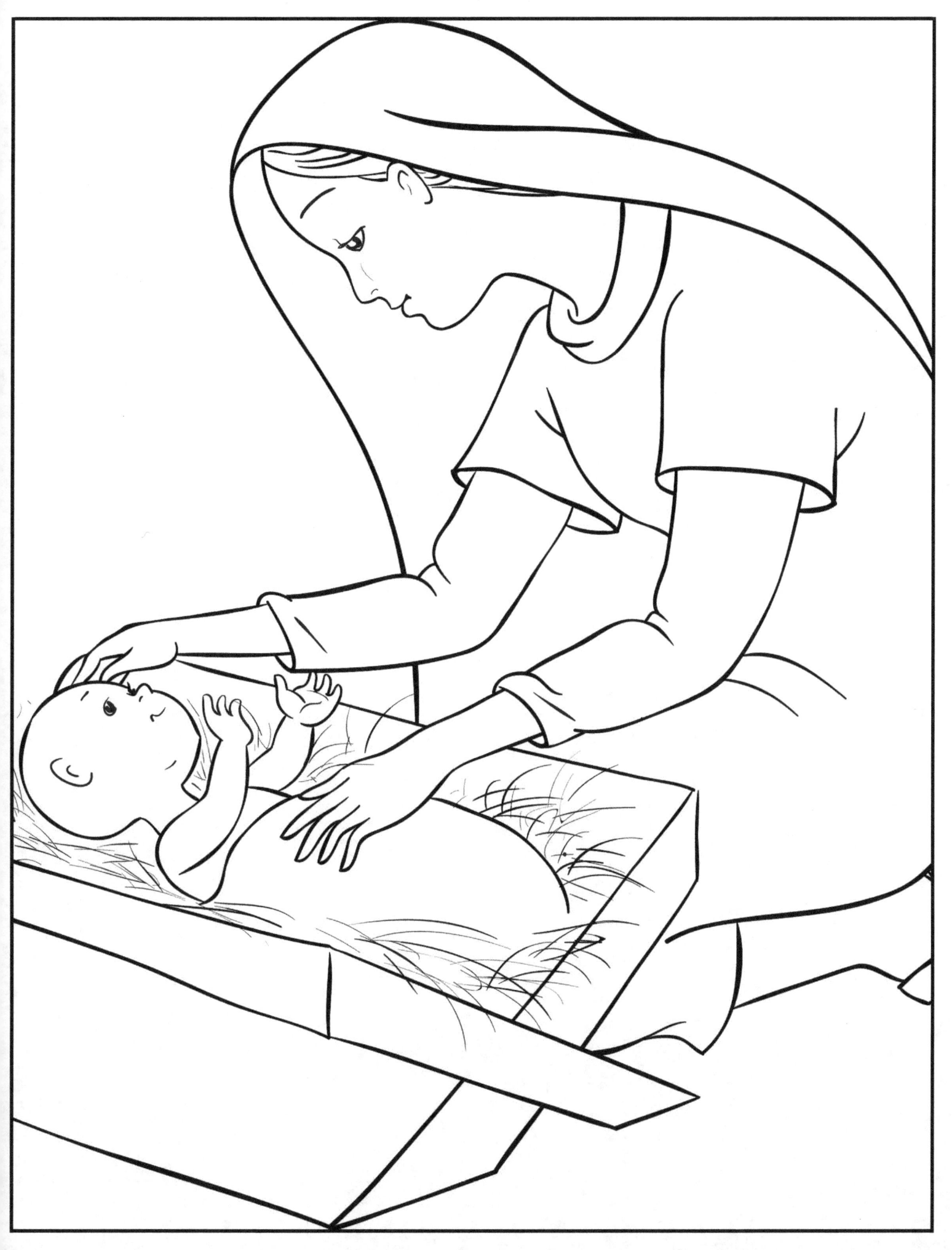

Copyright © 2017 by DP Kids
All rights reserved. This book or any portion thereof
may not be reproduced or used in any manner whatsoever without the express written permission of the publisher
except for the use of brief quotations in a book review.
First edition: 2017
Photo credit: Shutterstock
Disclaimer/Limit of Liability
This book is for informational purposes only. The views expressed are those of the author alone, and should not
be taken as expert, legal, or medical advice. The reader is responsible for his or her own actions.
Every attempt has been made to verify the accuracy of the information in this publication. However, neither the
author nor the publisher assumes any responsibility for errors, omissions, or contrary interpretation of the material
contained herein.

www.ingramcontent.com/pod-product-compliance
Lightning Source LLC
Chambersburg PA
CBHW081355080526
44588CB00016B/2506